An Insider's Secrets and Personalized Itinerary for an Unforgettable Vacation in 2023

Liverpool

Travel Guide
2023

Curtis Kerr

Table of Contents

X. CONCLUSION
Summary of The Guide

INTRODUCTION

Welcome to Liverpool

Liverpool, a city rich in culture, history, and a lively atmosphere, gladly welcomes visitors and gives them a warm welcome. You'll be enthralled by the vitality and charm that permeate the city the instant you step foot on its bustling streets.

An exhilaration swept over me as I strolled into Liverpool's busy streets. This exciting city had the promise of a great trip because of its fascinating history, legendary music culture, and hospitable residents. As people wandered around the shoreline, taking in the stunning architecture and humming bustle, laughing could be heard filling the air. I couldn't help but be drawn in by the spirit that filled every space.

I had always looked for uncommon locations that provided a combination of culture, entertainment, and undiscovered gems since I am an ardent traveler and self-proclaimed adventurer. Liverpool was the ideal place for my adventurous spirit because of its rich musical history and obvious attractiveness. I was eager to learn the unseen tales and inner secrets that were said to be waiting for me.

I set out on a trip to uncover Liverpool's actual essence equipped with a customized plan and a handbook full of insider information. My goal was to fully immerse myself in the city's spirit and make lifelong memories. This included touring the iconic Beatles locations and indulging in the local cuisine.

With its promise of life-changing events, Liverpool appealed to me, and I happily accepted. I had no idea that this metropolis would rob me of my heart and permanently alter my soul. As the days went by, I began to understand that Liverpool was more than simply a place to go; it was a magnificent world just waiting to be discovered, a location where dreams and realities came together in perfect harmony.

Get ready to get swept up in the fascinating fabric of Liverpool's history and present. The city has an unrivaled musical tradition that can be heard in every note played and every lyric sung since it is the home of the iconic Beatles. Prepare to explore the renowned Cavern Club and delve into The Beatles Story museum while following in the footsteps of these legendary artists.

The magnificent buildings of Liverpool are another pleasure to see. The magnificent Royal Liver Building and the Albert Dock serve as reminders of the city's rich maritime history, while the enormous Liverpool Cathedral inspires awe in all who see it. Take a leisurely walk along the charming waterfront, where modernism and tradition coexist peacefully while providing beautiful vistas and a lively environment.

As you sample the tastes of classic Scouse cuisine and learn about a dynamic culinary scene that appeals to all palates, be ready for a gourmet trip. Liverpool will tickle your taste senses and leave you wanting more with its unique cafés and acclaimed eateries.

Liverpool is unique because of its monuments and food, but it's also because of its residents' kind nature and contagious attitude. Liverpudlians are known for being amiable and funny, and they are always prepared to greet you with open arms, ensuring that your stay here is full of laughter, interesting discussions, and a feeling of belonging.

So, whether you're a fan of music, history, or culture, or just looking for a lively and fascinating experience, Liverpool is impatiently awaiting your visit. In this city of dreams, where magic comes to life and memorable moments are waiting to be formed, be ready to make lifetime memories. Greetings from Liverpool!

About This Guide

The Liverpool Travel Guide 2023: An Insider's Guide and Customized Itinerary for an Unforgettable Vacation is here to welcome you. Your go-to resource for experiencing Liverpool's dynamic city and discovering its hidden jewels in this guide.

This book combines insider advice, local suggestions, and a customized itinerary to give you a thorough and immersive experience, ensuring that your trip to Liverpool is nothing short of spectacular.

This book stands out by emphasizing insider information. We think that learning from and learning from individuals who live in a city is the greatest way to get to know it. We've compiled a list of insider tips that will enable you to see Liverpool like a real local, including lesser-known sights, neighborhood hangouts, secret restaurants, and off-the-beaten-path activities.

This book includes a well-planned schedule that may be altered to fit your tastes and interests in addition to insider advice. Whether you're a history buff itching to delve into the city's nautical heritage, a music fan seeking to discover the legacy of the Beatles, or a foodie seeking out gastronomic pleasures, our itinerary offers a framework for your experiences while allowing for flexibility and customization.

This book gives you all the resources you need to traverse Liverpool with comfort and confidence, including helpful information on travel necessities, suggested lodgings, transit alternatives, and language guidance.

Prepare to travel around Liverpool's lively streets, get engrossed in its cultural tapestry, and learn the secrets that make this city so unique. Let this book be your travel companion as you make priceless memories and discover Liverpool's enchantment like no before.

How to Use of This Guide

The purpose of this Liverpool travel guide 2023: An Insider's Secrets and Customized Itinerary for an Unforgettable Vacation is to improve your experience and provide you with the knowledge you need to make the most of your trip to Liverpool. The following advice will help you utilize this manual efficiently:

Prepare Yourself: To have a basic idea of everything Liverpool has to offer, start by reading this guide from beginning to finish. You'll have a better understanding of the city's attractions and features as a result.

Customize Your Itinerary: As a starting point, use the customizable itinerary offered in this handbook. By choosing the sights, events, and dining establishments that most appeal to you, you may personalize them to suit your interests and tastes. You are allowed to include or exclude elements to make a timetable that works for you.

Explore Insider Secrets: Pay close attention to the parts that feature insider information and undiscovered treasures. With the help of these insights, you'll be able to explore Liverpool beyond the conventional tourist attractions and find locally treasured unique experiences.

Plan Ahead: Write down useful information like available transit alternatives, suggested lodgings, and money-saving advice. This will enable you to organize your logistics in advance and guarantee a simple and affordable journey.

While this book offers a thorough overview, don't be afraid to stray from the established road and go exploring on your own. Engage the community, explore fresh eateries and coffee shops, and welcome unforeseen discoveries. The experiences that aren't included in the guidebook may sometimes be the finest ones.

Keep the Guide Close by Bring this guide with you on your vacation, whether it be in paper or digital form. It will be a handy resource for directions, phone numbers, and suggestions anytime you need them. The finest experiences are the ones you design for yourself; keep in mind that this guide is intended to be a useful resource. Accept the challenge, be receptive to new encounters, and make the most of your stay in Liverpool. Have fun on your trip!

How to Get Liverpool

Liverpool is well-connected and simple to get there via a variety of transportation options. Here are a few typical methods for getting to Liverpool:

- **By Air:** Liverpool John Lennon Airport (LPL) is the main airport servicing Liverpool and is situated approximately 7 miles from the city center. With links to significant cities in the UK and Europe, it provides both domestic and international flights. You may use cabs, buses, or trains to get to the city center from the airport.

- **In a train:** Liverpool Lime Street Station: One of the city's main rail hubs, Liverpool Lime Street offers direct links to several UK destinations. Train service to and from

Manchester, London, and other significant cities is excellent.

- **By Car:** Road networks: Liverpool is accessible by significant highways such as the M62, M6, and M58, which link the city to other UK regions. Plan your route properly since peak-period traffic congestion is a possibility.

- **By Bus:** Bus services are available from numerous UK cities to Liverpool via National Express and other bus companies. Due to its handy location, passengers may easily access Liverpool One, the bus terminal.

- **By Ferry:** There are ferry services connecting Liverpool and the Isle of Man, Dublin, and Belfast. The famous Pier Head, which is near the city center, is where the Liverpool Ferry Terminal is located.

Once you've arrived in Liverpool, you can easily get about and experience the city and its surroundings thanks to the city's well-connected public transit system, which includes buses and trains. Additionally accessible for easy city transport are taxis and ride-sharing services.

To guarantee a seamless and comfortable arrival in Liverpool, make your travel arrangements in advance, taking into account variables like travel duration, cost, and convenience.

How to Navigate Liverpool

You can get about Liverpool and experience its sights via a range of transportation methods. Here are a few typical transportation options in Liverpool:

- **Walking**: Liverpool's city center is relatively small and pedestrian-friendly, so seeing the top sights on foot is a great option. The Cavern Club, Liverpool ONE, and the Albert Dock are just a few of the well-known sites that are close to one another.

- **Public Buses:** Arriva and Stagecoach are only two of the many bus companies that operate in Liverpool. Buses provide handy transportation to several locations across the city and its adjacent regions. Tickets may be bought from the driver directly or via contactless payment options.

- **Merseyrail:** The Merseyrail network links to the larger Merseyside area and offers train services inside Liverpool. The Northern Line and the Wirral Line are the two lines that make up the network. Trains operate regularly and provide an effective means of getting throughout the city.

- **Taxis:** You may hail a taxi on the street or locate one at designated taxi ranks. Taxis are widely accessible around Liverpool. In the city, authorized black cabs and private rental cars are in use. It's best to utilize authorized taxis, negotiate the fee before the trip, or use the meter.

- **Bike rental:** Liverpool provides short-term bicycle rentals via bike-sharing programs including CityBike and Santander Cycles. You may ride these bikes to explore Liverpool at your leisure; you can find them at docking stations across the city.

- **Ferries:** The recognizable Mersey Ferries run frequent crossings of the River Mersey and provide picturesque views of the waterfront. For a leisurely sightseeing experience, you may take a ferry to places like the Wirral

Peninsula or even join a River Explorer Cruise.

- **Car Rental:** If you prefer the freedom of driving, Liverpool offers car rental options. However, bear in mind that parking in the city center may be scarce and expensive, so if you want to visit places outside of the city center, it may be worthwhile to take this alternative into account.

Liverpool has a variety of alternatives to fit various interests and budgets, whether you decide to walk, utilize public transportation, or use other modes of transportation to get about. To make your travels in Liverpool easy and pleasurable, plan your routes, review the schedules for public transportation, and think about utilizing mobile applications for real-time information.

Visa Requirements

Depending on your country, the reason for your visit, and how long you want to remain, Liverpool may need a visa. The following are some general principles:

Citizens of the European Union (EU) and the European Economic Area (EEA) are exempt from visa requirements while traveling to or staying in Liverpool or the United Kingdom (UK). This includes the citizens of Switzerland. A valid passport or national identification card is required to enter.

Visa Waiver Program (VWP) Countries: People from a select group of nations, including those in the US, Canada, Australia, New Zealand, Japan, South Korea, and many more, are permitted visa-free entry into the UK for up to six months as tourists. However, before your journey, you may need to apply for an Electronic Visa Waiver (EVW) or receive an Electronic Travel Authorization (ETA).

Non-Visa Waiver Program Countries: Before visiting Liverpool or the UK, citizens of nations not covered by the VWP will likely need to apply for a Standard Visitor Visa. An application must be submitted, supporting documentation must be provided, and a visa appointment must be attended at a UK embassy or consulate in your country of residence.

To find out the precise visa requirements depending on your nationality and situation, you must visit the official UK government website or speak with the closest UK embassy or consulate in your country. It's important to remain up to speed with the most recent information since visa restrictions and criteria might change.

Please be aware that this answer only offers broad information and suggestions on Liverpool's visa requirements. It is always advised to contact official government sources or ask for guidance from the appropriate authorities if you want reliable and extensive information about your particular situation.

Weather and Climate

Liverpool has a warm maritime climate with chilly summers and pleasant winters. Here is a description of Liverpool's climate and weather patterns:

Spring (March to May): Liverpool's springs are typically pleasant, with steadily increasing temperatures. Between March and May, daytime highs vary from around 8°C (46°F) to 15°C (59°F). Layers are advised since the weather may change quickly and there can be a few showers.

Summer (June to August): Compared to other regions of the UK, Liverpool's summers are often pleasant and comparatively cold. The average daily high and low are 17°C (63°F) and 20°C (68°F), respectively. Even while summers are often beautiful, it's a good idea to take a lightweight rain jacket or umbrella since they frequently rain.

Autumn (September to November): Liverpool's autumn is known for its warm weather and changing foliage. Around 17°C (63°F) in September and 10°C (50°F) in November are the average daily temperatures. Considering that rain is frequent at this time of year, it is wise to wear proper clothes and footwear.

Winter (December to February): Liverpool has chilly, rainy winters with temperatures between 6 and 9 degrees Celsius (43 and 48 degrees Fahrenheit). It may be windy, and there may sometimes be snow or frost, although it is usually not too bad. It is advised to wear warm clothing and be ready for rain.

Liverpool's climate is influenced by its closeness to the shore, which results in generally warm and temperate weather throughout the year. However, because weather conditions might vary, it's always a good idea to check the forecast before your journey.

Consider packing layers and having adequate gear for various circumstances, including a light rain jacket or umbrella. Keep in mind that weather patterns might vary.

Money and Currency Issues

The British Pound Sterling (£) is the currency used in Liverpool and the rest of the United Kingdom. Here are some details on money and currencies in Liverpool:

Exchange of Currencies: Liverpool's banks, exchange bureaus, and certain hotels all provide currency conversion to British Pounds. To be sure you're getting the greatest bargain, it's a good idea to check exchange rates and costs. Additionally, ATMs are extensively dispersed across the city, enabling you to withdraw money using your debit or credit card in the local currency.

Credit and Debit Cards: The majority of Liverpool's businesses, including hotels, eateries, stores, and attractions, accept credit and debit cards. American Express and Discover may be accepted to a lesser extent than Visa and Mastercard. To prevent any problems with card transactions, it's usually a good idea to let your bank or card provider know about your vacation intentions.

Despite the widespread acceptance of card payments, it is always a good idea to have some cash on hand for smaller businesses, neighborhood markets, and other locations that may not take cards. There are ATMs spread all around the city where you may get cash in British Pounds. To find out whether there are any fees associated with cash withdrawals, check with your bank. Keep in mind that certain ATMs may impose them.

Tipping: Tipping is expected but not required in Liverpool. If you have excellent service at a restaurant or pub, it's customary to give a tip that amounts to 10% to 15% of the tab. Before leaving a bigger tip, be sure there isn't a service fee at the restaurant. It is customary to round up taxi fares or provide a modest gratuity.

Budgeting: Depending on your tastes and hobbies, the cost of living in Liverpool might change. Budget between £80 to £120 per day, on average, for midrange lodging, food, local transportation, and attractions. However, depending on your purchasing patterns and preferred degree of luxury, this may change.

Take the required security measures for your money and possessions, as you would in any city. Use safe ATMs and keep a watch on your possessions, particularly in busy places. Having a backup strategy, such as retaining copies of crucial papers and having access to emergency finances, is also a good idea.

Before your journey to Liverpool, it's a good idea to check the exchange rates and speak with your bank or financial institution to get the most recent information and guidance on currency exchange and financial problems.

Language and Communication Tips

English is widely used as a first language in Liverpool and the rest of the United Kingdom.

Here are some details on communication and language in Liverpool:

English is widely spoken and understood by the vast majority of Liverpool residents. Communicating in English will usually be adequate, whether you're engaging with people, asking for help, or visiting tourist sites.

Scouse Dialect: In Liverpool, you can encounter a distinctive regional accent and dialect known as "Scouse." Scouse is a dialect of the English language with its distinctive pronunciation, vocabulary, and idioms. While it could take some getting used to, most residents will use basic English while speaking with tourists.

Foreign Languages: You could run across people who can speak Spanish, French, German, or Mandarin in touristy neighborhoods and institutions. But in Liverpool, English continues to be the major language of communication.

Communication Advice: To guarantee comprehension, it's best to talk slowly and clearly while speaking with natives. Never be reluctant to seek assistance or ask questions if you need it. The people of Liverpool are often affable and kind.

Public signage is mostly in English, including street signs, transit signs, and tourist information. Especially at important sites, you could see signs in many languages in well-known tourist locations.

Tools for Language Translation: If you'd want some help communicating during your visit, you may utilize mobile applications or online translation services. These resources may be used to translate written text or simple phrases.

Overall, Liverpool's primary language of communication is English. However, to be respectful and improve your relationships with locals, it's always a good idea to learn a few fundamental English phrases and pleasantries.

Emergency Numbers and Safety Tips in Liverpool

Although it's typically safe to go to Liverpool, you should always take steps to protect your safety and well-being. Keep in mind the following safety advice and emergency phone numbers:

Personal Security

- Be mindful of your surroundings, particularly when it's busy or late at night.

- Be cautious of pickpockets and keep your stuff safe, particularly in popular tourist places.

- Keep valuable objects and significant sums of money hidden from view.

- When strolling at night, stick to crowded, well-lit areas.

- Inform someone of your intentions and anticipated return time if you are heading out.

Transport Security:

- Avoid getting into unmarked or unauthorized cars and instead use authorized taxis or reliable ride-sharing services.

- Be watchful of your valuables and alert to any strange behavior around you while utilizing public transit.

Emergency Contacts

- Call 999 for quick help in an emergency. For police, fire, and medical situations, dial this number.

- If you need non-emergency help or guidance, call the local police at (911) 101.

Medical and Health:

- Liverpool has several hospitals and medical facilities, including the Royal Liverpool University Hospital and the Liverpool Heart and Chest Hospital, if you need medical attention.

- It is advised to get travel insurance that includes emergency medical evacuation and coverage for medical costs.

Respect local customs and laws:

- To guarantee that you abide by rules and show respect for local culture, familiarize yourself with the laws and traditions of the area.

- Pay close attention to any particular rules or limits at tourist locations as well as any safety advice given by authorities.

Stay Up to Date:

- Keep up on neighborhood news and travel warnings both before and during your trip to Liverpool.

- Observe any safety recommendations or warnings provided by regional authorities.

- You should always use common sense, follow your intuition, and take appropriate steps to guarantee your safety and security when traveling. Keep in mind that these safety advice are broad recommendations.

Accommodation Options and Liverpool's Best Hotels

Liverpool has a variety of lodging choices to accommodate various spending limits and tastes. You can discover lodging to suit your requirements, whether you're seeking five-star resorts, upscale inns, or inexpensive hostels. Here are some of the best hotels in Liverpool, along with information:

1. Liverpool's Titanic Hotel:

Stanley Dock is at Regent Road in Liverpool, England, L3 0AN.
The Titanic Hotel provides opulent suites with industrial-chic design and is housed in a former warehouse in the famous Stanley Dock. The hotel has roomy accommodations, a chic restaurant, a

spa, and a rooftop terrace with magnificent city views.

2. The Shankly Hotel:

Location: 60 Victoria Street, Liverpool L1 6JD, Millennium House
The Shankly Hotel is a football-themed lodging honoring the late Bill Shankly, manager of Liverpool FC. The hotel has chic accommodations, a rooftop bar, and a museum filled with football-related artifacts. It is situated in the center of the city, close to popular tourist destinations and commercial centers.

3. The Malmaison

Address: 7 William Jessop Way, Liverpool, England, L3 1QZ
The Malmaison provides contemporary rooms with sleek and modern decor and is located on the

riverfront near Princes Dock. The hotel has a chic bistro, a bar, and a fitness center. It provides breathtaking views of the Mersey River and is close to landmarks like the Albert Dock.

4. The Hard Days Night Hotel:

North John Street, Liverpool, L2 6RR
In the center of Liverpool is where you'll find this hotel with a Beatles motif. The Hard Days Night Hotel has a restaurant, a bar, and a music-themed lounge in addition to specially designed rooms that were inspired by the well-known band. Popular destinations including Liverpool ONE and the Cavern Club are close by.

5. Hope Street Hotel:

40 Hope Street, Liverpool, L1 9DA
The Hope Street Hotel, located in the hip Georgian Quarter, provides boutique lodging in a fashionable

and opulent environment. The hotel has uniquely designed guest rooms, a restaurant providing food made with fresh local ingredients, and a rooftop terrace with expansive city views.

These are just a handful of the finest Liverpool hotels that come highly rated. The Vincent Hotel, 30 James Street, the location of the Titanic, and the Hilton Liverpool City Centre are further noteworthy choices. To pick the hotel that best meets your requirements and tastes, it is advised to compare costs, check for availability, and read reviews.

III. EXPLORING LIVERPOOL

History of Liverpool

Over 800 years of history have passed in Liverpool, making it a city with a rich and varied past. Liverpool has made a huge contribution to defining the history of the United Kingdom and the rest of the globe from its modest origins as a tiny fishing hamlet to becoming one of the largest port cities in the world. Here is a detailed account of Liverpool's history:

Ancient Years:
Ancient villages and Viking activities provide evidence of human occupation in the region where Liverpool currently sits stretching back thousands of years. Liverpool was a little fishing and trade settlement in the 12th century known as "Liuerpul," which translates to "muddy creek" or "pool with muddy water."

The Slave Trade and Port City:
When Liverpool got engaged in the transatlantic slave trade and started importing products from Africa and the Americas, it started to develop into a significant port. The port of the city had great growth in the 18th and 19th centuries, contributing to its importance as a trading and industrial center for the British Empire.

Industrial and Maritime Expansion:
The world's first commercial wet dock's completion in 1715 was a crucial turning point in Liverpool's maritime history. Liverpool, which served as a significant commercial hub for cotton imports and exports throughout the 18th and 19th centuries, was critical to the development of the cotton industry.

Liverpool's commerce and connections were significantly bolstered by the railroad's early 19th-century advent.

Heritage in the Arts and Culture:

Liverpool has made significant contributions to music, literature, and athletics, and it has a rich cultural and creative history. The Beatles, who achieved worldwide recognition in the 1960s, were among the well-known artists that the city is known for producing. Many famous monuments may be found in Liverpool, including the Royal Liver Building, the Cavern Club, and the World Museum.

Second World War and Post-War Recovery:

Due to its important port position, Liverpool saw intense bombing during World War II, causing major city damage and human casualties. New housing estates and the development of the city's infrastructure were the results of post-war rehabilitation and urban growth.

Cultural and Modern Revitalization Capital of Europe

When Liverpool was named the 2008 European Capital of Culture, there was a considerable increase in funding for the arts, culture, and urban renewal. With the creation of waterfront attractions, the preservation of historic structures, and the expansion of the tourist and leisure sectors, the city experienced substantial redevelopment.

Liverpool is known for its rich history, architectural legacy, world-class museums, flourishing music scene, and illustrious football teams today. The city is also known for its dynamic and diverse atmosphere. Visitors from all over the world find it to be a fascinating destination because of its maritime history, cultural variety, and continuing development.

Note: The history of Liverpool is outlined above in broad strokes. It is advised to consult historical texts, regional archives, and historical-focused institutions for a more thorough understanding.

Liverpool Today

The northwest English city of Liverpool is a thriving, culturally diversified metropolis with a lot to offer. Here is a current-day overview of Liverpool:

Industry and the economy:
Over time, Liverpool's economy has become more diverse. The city has seen an expansion in several sectors, including banking, education, tourism, creative arts, and digital technology, even though the port still plays a large role. Major investments have been drawn to the Liverpool City Region, resulting in the growth of commercial and economic sectors including Liverpool Waters and the Knowledge Quarter.

Vacationing and Attractions

Liverpool is a well-known travel destination that draws many tourists each year. Numerous attractions are available in the city, including the UNESCO-designated World Heritage Site that includes its historic waterfront.

A popular tourist destination, the Albert Dock has restaurants, boutiques, art galleries, museums, and more. Popular cultural destinations include Tate Liverpool, the Merseyside Maritime Museum, and the Beatles Story Museum. Liverpool is renowned for having a thriving music culture with several live music venues and events all year long.

Entertainment, Culture, and the Arts

A vibrant arts and cultural scene exists in the city. The Everyman and Playhouse Theatres provide a range of plays and shows, while the Liverpool Philharmonic Hall presents concerts of classical music. The Walker Art Gallery, the Bluecoat, as well as other smaller galleries and street art exhibits, all honor the city's creative past.

The Liverpool International Music Festival, the Liverpool Comedy Festival, and the Liverpool Biennial, a festival of contemporary art, are just a few of the yearly events that take place in Liverpool.

Education & Innovation
Universities like the University of Liverpool, Liverpool John Moores University, and Liverpool Hope University are well-known in Liverpool. The intellectual and research landscape of the city is influenced by these institutions.

With programs like the Liverpool Science Park and the Sensor City innovation hub, the city promotes innovation and entrepreneurship and draws tech businesses and cross-disciplinary research partnerships.

Sports:

Liverpool's culture has a unique place for football. Two well-known football teams, Liverpool FC and Everton FC, with fervent fan bases and a long-standing rivalry, call the city home.
Football fans from all over the globe go to Anfield Stadium and Goodison Park, while the city's athletic grounds also hold other events including rugby games and concerts.

Delicious Food and Nightlife:
With a variety of exotic cuisines, classic English pubs, and hip eateries, Liverpool has a vibrant food culture. Local products and street cuisine are featured at the city's food markets, including the Baltic Market and the Liverpool Cuisine and Drink Festival.

Liverpool has a thriving nightlife with many pubs, clubs, and live music venues. The vibrant nightlife in places like Mathew Street and the Baltic Triangle is well-known. Liverpool is a modern metropolis that blends its extensive heritage with cutting-edge advancements. It is an attractive location for locals and tourists alike because of its thriving cultural scene, economic prosperity, and welcoming attitude.

Exploring Liverpool's Top Attractions

Liverpool is a bustling city with a rich cultural history and beautiful architecture. Liverpool offers something for everyone, whether you like music, history, art, or just adore discovering new places. Here is a detailed list of Liverpool's main attractions:

1. Albert Dock:

The Albert Dock is a historic collection of dock buildings that is now home to several attractions. It is situated on the riverfront of the UNESCO World Heritage Site.

- Learn more about the most well-known band in the world by visiting The Beatles Story, or take a look at Liverpool's nautical past by visiting the Merseyside Nautical Museum.

- The International Slavery Museum offers details on the city's history in the transatlantic slave trade, while the Tate Liverpool art museum exhibits modern and contemporary art.

2. The Beatles Story and The Cavern Club

- Visit The Beatles Story to fully immerse yourself in The Beatles' history. You are taken on a trip through the lives and songs of the renowned band via this interactive museum.

- Visit the Cavern Club on Mathew Street, where The Beatles memorably gave early performances. Take in the energetic environment while listening to live music.

3. St. George's Hall and the Liverpool Cathedral:

- One of the most recognizable buildings in the city is the Liverpool Cathedral. To fully appreciate its magnificent design and ascend the tower for sweeping views of the city, take a guided tour.

- In the center of the city stands the majestic neoclassical structure known as St. George's Hall. Discover its opulent interiors and go to performances and exhibits.

4 . The Pier Head and Royal Albert Dock:

- At the Royal Albert Dock, wander along the lovely waterfront. Take in the views of the Three Graces—the Royal Liver Building, the Cunard Building, and the Port of Liverpool Building—while eating on the waterfront and shopping in upscale stores.

- Don't forget to see the iconic "Liver Birds" that is perched atop the Royal Liver Building.

5. The World Museum and The Walker Art Gallery:

Impressive collections of European paintings, sculptures, and decorative arts are kept in the Walker Art Gallery. Reputable painters like Rembrandt, Monet, and Hockney have pieces there.

The World Museum has a wide variety of exhibitions, such as displays of natural history and a planetarium, as well as antiquities from ancient Egypt.

6. Goodison Park and Anfield Stadium:

- Football lovers should visit Liverpool FC's Anfield Stadium and take a guided tour to see the facility, trophy room, and club history.

- Take a tour of Goodison Park, the home of Everton FC, to feel the atmosphere and discover more about this illustrious football team.

7. The Liverpool Central Library and The Bluecoat

A stunning 18th-century structure serves as the home of the modern arts complex known as The Bluecoat. It sponsors exhibits, performances, and seminars that include both domestic and foreign talent.

The Liverpool Central Library is a magnificent piece of architecture. Visit literary events, peruse the library's extensive collection of books, or just unwind in the rooftop garden with its sweeping city views.

8. The Palm House and Sefton Park:

Sefton Park is a charming Victorian park with lovely scenery, lakes, and a boating lake where you can get away from the rush and bustle of the city.

The Palm House is a charming glasshouse with exotic plants located within the park. Enjoy the peaceful surroundings by taking a leisurely walk.

These are just a handful of Liverpool's major tourist destinations. The city has a lot to offer, from discovering its musical legacy to learning about its maritime past and taking in its thriving cultural scene. Spend some time exploring and discovering everything that Liverpool has to offer.

Hidden Gems and Local Favorites

Liverpool has several well-known attractions, but it also has some undiscovered jewels and neighborhood favorites that provide special experiences off the main route. Here are some Liverpool hidden treasures and neighborhood hotspots to check out:

1. The Baltic Triangle

The independent galleries, street art, music venues, and fashionable pubs in this thriving creative neighborhood are well-known. To fully experience Liverpool's alternative arts and cultural scene, go there.

2 . St. Luke's Cathedral

This largely ruined chapel, which is in the heart of the city, currently serves as an outdoor location for markets, gatherings, and performances. It is a moving reminder of Liverpool's tenacity during World War II.

3. Lark Lane

Lark Lane, a bohemian lane filled with oddball stores, independent boutiques, quaint cafés, and vibrant pubs, is tucked away in the neighborhood of Aigburth. Locals like it because of the relaxed ambiance and exciting nightlife.

4. The Philharmonic Dining Rooms:

As you enter this magnificent Victorian bar, you'll be astounded by the sumptuous furnishings, which include stained-glass windows, mosaic flooring, and elaborate woodwork. Enjoy a pint of regional beer or try some classic pub fare.

5. Williamson Tunnels

Explore the maze of tunnels built by eccentric benefactor Joseph Williamson in the 19th century by venturing underneath the city. Learn about their enigmatic past and function by taking a tour.

6. The Florrie, The Florence Institute's

Formerly a boys' club, this Grade II listed structure in the Dingle area is now a gathering place for the locals. To get a sense of the active local culture, check out a concert, an exhibition of art, or a community function.

7. The Dead Crafty Brewery:

Beer lovers will like this welcoming craft beer pub hidden away on a side street. It's a terrific spot to try out uncommon brews and interact with welcoming people since it has a changing assortment of regional and foreign beers.

8. Crosby Beach and Antony Gormley Art Piece

Crosby Beach, which is just a short rail journey from the city center, has spectacular coastline views and Antony Gormley's art piece, which is made up of 100 cast-iron figures arranged along the beach.

9. St. George's District

Discover the architectural wonders of the ancient St. George's Quarter, including the neoclassical St. George's Hall, the World Museum, and the Central Library. Learn about the region's unique history by going on a guided walking tour.

10. The Liverpool Gin distillery:

Visit this undiscovered treasure housed in a historic Victorian factory. Take a tour, taste several gins, and savor handmade cocktails while learning about the gin-making process.

Beyond the well-known attractions, these undiscovered jewels and neighborhood favorites provide an insight into the varied and lively culture of Liverpool. Spend some time exploring these less-traveled areas to get a true sense of the neighborhood and the city's distinctive character.

Galleries and Museums

The museums and galleries in Liverpool contribute significantly to the preservation and promotion of the history, art, and maritime legacy of the city. Liverpool is home to a rich cultural heritage. The best museums and art galleries in Liverpool are listed below:

The Beatles Story: The Beatles Story, located near the Albert Dock, is a must-see for any admirer of the Fab Four. This interactive museum uses displays, artifacts, and audio-visual presentations to chronicle the history of the legendary band.

The Museum of Liverpool: The Museum of Liverpool, which is located on the waterfront, covers the rich legacy and history of the city. Learn about Liverpool's history, from its early days to its contributions to the industrial revolution, maritime commerce, and popular culture.

The Merseyside Maritime Museum: The Merseyside Maritime Museum, which is also in the Albert Dock, explores Liverpool's maritime history. Discover historical maritime exhibitions about the Titanic, the Atlantic Battle, and the city's involvement in the slave trade.

Tate Liverpool: The Tate Liverpool exhibitions modern and contemporary art as a member of the Tate network. It presents recurring shows that include pieces created by well-known international artists. Awe-inspiring views of the waterfront are also available from the gallery.

Walker Gallery of Art: The city's cultural district is home to the Walker Art Gallery, which has a sizable collection of artwork from various periods.

Admire current artworks as well as masterpieces from British and European masters.

World Museum: All ages will find the World Museum to be intriguing due to its wide variety of exhibits. Learn about space and astronomy, take in the exhibits of natural history, and discover past civilizations.

The International Slavery Museum: The International Slavery Museum, which is located near the Albert Dock, offers compelling insights into the transatlantic slave trade and its effects on Liverpool and the rest of the globe. It examines topics from the past and the present about slavery and its repercussions.

The Victoria Gallery and Museum: The Victoria Gallery & Museum, which is a part of the University of Liverpool, is home to an intriguing collection of works of art, antiques, and oddities.

Discover its diverse exhibits, which include Victorian art, medical items, and a lovely performance space.

The Bluecoat: A modern arts facility called The Bluecoat is situated in a landmark structure. It offers a variety of performances, exhibits, and events that highlight regional and worldwide artists working in a range of artistic mediums.

The Open Eye Gallery: The Open Eye Gallery is devoted to photography and hosts provocative exhibits and initiatives that examine the many genres, methods, and societal implications of the medium.

Explore Liverpool's maritime heritage or immerse yourself in modern art at one of the many museums and galleries the city has to offer. These institutions provide an enthralling look into Liverpool's rich cultural fabric, whether you're interested in history, music, art, or cultural heritage.

Discover Liverpool's Parks and Gardens

Liverpool is renowned for its lovely parks and gardens in addition to its bustling urban landscape. These green areas provide a calm respite from the bustle of the city and chances for leisure, entertainment, and appreciation of nature. Here is a detailed guide to visiting Liverpool's parks and gardens:

Sefton Park

- With a total area of 235 acres, Sefton Park is one of Liverpool's biggest and most well-liked parks. It has lakes, meadows, wonderfully planted gardens, and even a palm house.

- Visit the lake in a rowboat or take a leisurely walk along the meandering trails. You can even enjoy a picnic on the lush meadows. Events and exhibits are often held in the magnificent glass building known as The Palm House, which houses exotic plants.

Calderstones Park:

- Calderstones Park in south Liverpool is a tranquil haven with a fascinating past. The Calderstones, ancient megaliths from the Neolithic era, may be found in the park.

- Visit the Mansion House, which has a café and a historical center, and explore the exquisitely kept grounds, stroll through the Japanese-inspired garden, and other areas.

Country Park and Croxteth Hall:

- Within a vast rural park sits the majestic stately mansion Croxteth Hall. Explore the hall's opulent interiors and stroll around the expansive parks, forests, and gardens.

- In addition to horseback riding, cycling, and walking pathways are also available in the park. The Victorian Walled Garden, where you may enjoy lovely flowers and vegetables, should not be missed.

Otterspool Park and promenade:

- Otterspool Park, which is located along the Mersey River's banks, provides breathtaking views of both the river and the Wirral Peninsula. There are open green areas, playgrounds, and a promenade in the park.

- Have a picnic, take a leisurely bike ride along the promenade, or watch the sunset over the river. All year long, the park also holds festivals and events.

Stanley Park

- An attractive Victorian park called Stanley Park is close to Anfield Stadium. It has stunning scenery, a lake with rowing boats, and an impressive pavilion.

- Visit the Isla Gladstone Conservatory, a popular location for gatherings and weddings that features a glass conservatory surrounded by lovely gardens. Tennis courts and a track are among the sporting amenities in the park.

Greenbank Park:

- Greenbank Park, a tranquil environment with well-kept gardens, flowerbeds, and a lovely lake, is found in the Mossley Hill neighborhood.

- Wander through the park at your own pace, have a picnic on the grass, or just unwind on a seat. Tennis courts and a children's play area are also included in the park.

Newsham Park

- A historic park with large green areas, wooded areas, and a lovely lake is called Newsham Park. With playgrounds, sporting venues, and picnic spots, it's a terrific destination for a family day.

- The Grade II listed Newsham Park Hospital, a former workhouse that now houses flats, is also located in the park. Enjoy the tranquil settings and the park's heritage.

Princes Park:

- A charming Victorian park called Princes Park may be found close to Toxteth. It has lovely gardens, a lake, and a path around the park.

- Make use of the park's trails to jog or slowly stroll while taking in the flower displays and the tranquil ambiance.

These Liverpool parks and gardens provide a welcome respite from the bustle of the city. These green areas provide a pleasant sanctuary for all guests to enjoy, whether they're looking for peace, a location for outdoor activities, or just to connect with nature.

Shopping in Liverpool

Liverpool is a bustling shopping destination with a variety of stores to suit all interests and inclinations. The city offers something for everyone, from high-end designer stores to vintage shops and active markets. The following is a detailed guide to shopping in Liverpool:

Liverpool ONE

- In the center of the city, Liverpool ONE is a major retail destination. More than 170 high-street brands, department shops, and designer boutiques are represented there.

- Discover the open-air retail center's contemporary design and renowned architecture. Learn about well-known fashion stores, beauty salons, electronics stores, and lifestyle companies.

Bold Street

- A busy street in the heart of the city, Bold Street is well-known for its independent stores, retro boutiques, and distinctive eateries. It's the ideal location for discovering eccentric clothing, vinyl music, books, and regional artwork.

- Discover the diverse assortment of stores and take in the lively ambiance of this bohemian shopping area.

Metquarter

- The Metquarter, which is a part of the Liverpool ONE complex, provides a more upscale retail experience. It has luxurious jewelry shops, spas, and high-end fashion labels.

- Explore premium brands, peruse high-end cosmetics, and reward yourself with a chic shopping experience.

Cave Walks

- Cavern Walks is a boutique retail arcade that is tucked away in the city's exclusive Ropewalks neighborhood. Exclusive fashion stores, independent designers, and stylish accessories may be found there.

- Discover the distinctive offers in fashion, from cutting-edge attire to opulent footwear and accessories.

Grand Central Hall

Grand Central Hall, which is housed in a gorgeous Victorian structure, is a hidden treasure for vintage and alternative shopping. It has vintage clothes shops, vinyl record stores, and oddball artifacts, and it often holds a vintage fair.

St. John's Shopping Centre

- One of Liverpool's oldest shopping centers, St. John's Shopping Centre has a wide variety of stores. It consists of independent merchants, well-known high-street names, and discount shops.

- Look through reasonably priced apparel, accessories, gadgets, and home products.

Pop-up Markets and Farmers' Markets:

- Liverpool is home to several bustling pop-ups and farmers' markets that sell handmade items, street cuisine, and fresh local vegetables.

- To enjoy the busy atmosphere and find unusual things, visit markets like the Granby Street Market, Baltic Market, and Liverpool Central Market.

Church Street

- Church Street is a prominent high-street shopping thoroughfare, department store, and retail chain situated in the heart of the city. It is a one-stop store for purchasing fashion, beauty products, and lifestyle items.

- Discover the colorful stores, benefit from the seasonal deals, and take in exciting street entertainment.

Lark Lane:

- Lark Lane in Aigburth, with its independent boutiques, vintage shops, and eccentric retailers, provides a bohemian shopping experience.

- Enjoy the relaxed ambiance of this colorful street while browsing unusual clothing, vintage treasures, artwork, and antiques.

Shopping at Designer Outlets:

- Designer outlets shopping facilities like Cheshire Oaks Designer Outlet and Liverpool Designer Shopping Outlet are located not far from Liverpool. These locations provide reduced pricing on designer clothing, luxury goods, and home goods.

- Liverpool's retail culture is broad and lively, with everything from contemporary shopping centers to small shops and marketplaces. You may discover whatever you're looking for in this vibrant city, including the newest fashion trends, one-of-a-kind vintage items, and regionally produced artisanal products.

Nightlife and Entertainment

Liverpool is famous for having a thriving entertainment and nightlife scene. The city has a variety of alternatives to suit every taste, from hip pubs and clubs to live music venues and theaters. Here is a thorough guide to enjoying Liverpool's nightlife and entertainment:

Concert Square:

- Concert Square, which lies in the heart of the city, is a bustling center for pubs and clubs. It's a well-liked hangout for anyone seeking a fun night out.

- Discover the numerous locations that feature a range of musical styles, from top songs to underground techno sounds. Drinks, dancing, and a lively environment are all welcome.

The Cavern Club:

- The Cavern Club is a legendary music venue well-known for being The Beatles' birthplace. It keeps showcasing live musical performers as a tribute to the city's musical history.

- As bands and artists hit the stage to play live for the audience, soak in the exciting atmosphere.

The Baltic Triangle

- A creative and cultural neighborhood called the Baltic Triangle is well-known for its exciting nightlife. There are several taverns, clubs, and music venues there.

- Explore distinctive venues that provide live DJ performances, alternative music genres, and immersive experiences. Discover Liverpool's nightlife's innovative and varied side.

The Philharmonic Dining Rooms:
- The Philharmonic Dining Rooms is a well-liked venue for listening to live music in addition to being a gorgeous Victorian tavern. Jazz evenings, classical music concerts, and other musical events are often held there.

- Enjoy the sounds of great musicians in a beautiful location as you sit back and relax.

Royal Court Theatre

- The Royal Court Theatre is a venerable venue where plays, comedies, musicals, and other acts are presented.

- Catch a performance to get a taste of the theater, which includes both traveling shows and regional ones.

Kazimier Garden

- Live music, DJ sets, and artistic performances may be seen in the distinctive outdoor venue known as The Kazimier Garden. It is renowned for its diverse activities and all-encompassing experiences.

- Experience the enchanted ambiance of this hidden treasure while taking in performances in a lovely garden setting.

- **Liverpool Empire Theatre:**

A variety of performances are presented in the majestic Liverpool Empire Theatre, including musicals, plays, ballets, and concerts. Enjoy the excitement of live concerts in a beautiful environment.

- **Comedy Clubs**

Liverpool is home to various comedy clubs, including Laughterhouse Comedy Club and Hot Water Comedy Club. These places host both well-known and rising comedians, making for hilarious nights.

- **Alma de Cuba**

In a former church, there is a unique bar and restaurant called Alma de Cuba. It provides a fun environment with live entertainment, beverages, and music with a Latin influence.

Enjoy the colorful spirit of this well-liked venue as you dance the night away to contagious beats.

- **Albert Dock**

In addition to being a popular daytime destination, Albert Dock is also a center for entertainment at night. It has live music venues, pubs, and dining establishments with a view of the sea. Drink in the stunning views while watching a show, attend a live show, or go to a comedy club for a fun night out.

There is always something for everyone to enjoy thanks to Liverpool's broad nightlife and entertainment scene. The city offers a variety of entertainment options, including live music, theater, comedy, and a vibrant club scene. Liverpool is a dynamic city where you can experience exciting nightlife and make lifelong memories.

IV. FOOD AND DRINK

Traditional Scouse Cuisine

Liverpool has its unique culinary traditions, and Scouse is among the most well-known foods connected to the city. Hearty stew known as scouse has long been a mainstay of Liverpool cuisine. Here are several classic foods that are well worth eating, including Scouse:

Scouse: Traditional ingredients for the meat and vegetable stew known as scouse include lamb or beef, potatoes, onions, and carrots. To make a food that is rich and savory, it is slowly cooked.

The word "Scouse" comes from the stew known as "lobscouse," which was a favorite among sailors. It often comes with crusty bread and pickled red cabbage or beets.

Liverpool's Pies: Liverpool's savory pies are renowned for their deliciousness. The most well-known of them is "Scouse pie," which encases the stew's tastes in pastry. It is a full and soothing meal.

Wet Nelly: A typical dessert from Liverpool is called Wet Nelly. A spoonful of custard or cream is often added to this rich, fruit-filled bread pudding before eating. The expression "wet and allez," which means moist and delectable, is said to have inspired the moniker "Wet Nelly".

Scouse Nans: A savory meat pie with a pastry crust is called a Scouse Nan. They are a common snack or lunch choice in Liverpool and are often packed with a combination of minced beef, onions, and potatoes.

Liverpool's Dry Gin: Liverpool has a distinctive gin, however, it's not a dish. Coriander, citrus, and juniper are among the botanicals used in Liverpool Gin, a premium gin. Gin lovers often choose it as a terrific method to get a flavor of Liverpool.

Lobster Pot: The Lobster Pot is a well-known seafood establishment in Liverpool that focuses on serving meals using fresh fish and shellfish. It's an excellent location to try regional seafood specialties including grilled fish, prawns, and oysters.

Butter Pie: A distinctive meal that is well-liked in the area is butter pie. It is a savory pie with a pastry shell with a filling of mashed potatoes, onions, and butter. It's an easy yet filling comfort dish.

Scouse Egg: An alternative to the standard Scotch egg is the Scouse Egg. It has a hard-boiled egg that has been wrapped in breadcrumbs, seasoned with minced beef, then deep-fried till golden and crispy. To experience Liverpool's rich culinary history, try these classic meals when you visit the city. Scouse stew, savory pies, and distinctive desserts are just a few of the mouthwatering dishes Liverpool's traditional cuisine has to offer.

Iconic Cafes & Restaurants in Liverpool

Liverpool has a thriving eating scene with a wide variety of renowned eateries and cafés that highlight the culinary brilliance of the city. Here are several well-known places worth visiting, serving anything from foreign food to classic British fare:

1. The Art School Restaurant

One Sugnall Street, Liverpool, England, L7 7EB Chef Paul Askew is the owner and head chef of the Michelin-starred The Art School Restaurant. It has an exceptional menu with contemporary British cuisine that emphasizes fresh, in-season ingredients. A unique dining experience is provided by the exquisite atmosphere and excellent service.

2. Hope Street

60 Hope Street, Liverpool, England, L1 9BZ
The Georgian townhouse-style restaurant 60 Hope Street combines elegant dining with bistro fare. The restaurant's menu combines contemporary British cuisine with tastes from throughout the world, all of which were lovingly and skillfully created. Its attraction is heightened by the lovely surroundings and gracious service.

3. London Carriage Works

40 Hope Street, Liverpool, England, L1 9DA
The London Carriage Works, a restaurant within the Hope Street Hotel, is well known for serving modern British cuisine. The restaurant takes pleasure in utilizing regional ingredients to make unique and flavorful meals. It's a well-liked option for both residents and tourists due to its chic décor and warm atmosphere.

4. The Philharmonic Dining Rooms

36 Hope Street, Liverpool, England, L1 9BX
The Philharmonic Dining Rooms is a classic bar with beautiful architecture and a long history. With an emphasis on traditional meals and a large range of ales and beers, it provides a genuine British pub experience. Its particular attractiveness is enhanced by the extravagant design, which includes its renowned gents' restrooms.

5. The Brunch Club

In Liverpool, England, at 37–41 Duke Street, L1 5AP
The Brunch Club is a well-liked eatery renowned for its delectable breakfast and brunch selections. There is something for every taste, from light pancakes and filling full English breakfasts to wholesome smoothie bowls and avocado toast. It is

a favorite among brunch lovers because of the laid-back ambiance and helpful staff.

6. The Leaf

Location: Liverpool, L1 4EZ, 65-67 Bold Street
The Leaf is a bustling tea store and café tucked away in the middle of Bold Street. Along with a range of sandwiches, salads, and light fare, it also has a big assortment of teas from all over the globe. A relaxed and welcoming ambiance is created by the diverse design, pleasant sitting spaces, and live music events.

7. The Baltic Social

27 Parliament Street, Liverpool, England L8 5RN
The Baltic Social is a hip restaurant in the Baltic Triangle neighborhood. It offers a variety of comfort foods, such as upscale burgers, stuffed fries, and decadent milkshakes. Its eccentric décor, which

includes old furniture and graffiti art, contributes to the atmosphere of chill and relaxation.

8. Mowgli Street Food

69 Bold Street, Liverpool, England L1 4EZ
An exciting and flavorful taste of India is offered by Mowgli Street Food. The menu offers a variety of small plates and meals with street cuisine inspiration that is brimming with flavor and scent. It is a preferred option for parties and food connoisseurs because of the vibrant ambiance and sharing-style eating.

These recognizable cafes and restaurants in Liverpool serve as a representation of the city's varied culinary scene and provide a variety of eating options, including both fine dining and fast food. If you're looking for

Local Pubs and Bars

Liverpool is well known for its thriving pub and bar culture, which has a variety of places that can accommodate a broad range of interests and preferences. Here are several neighborhood favorites worth checking out, ranging from classic pubs to modern cocktail bars:

1. Ye Cracke

13 Rice Street, Liverpool, England, L1 9BB
Famous people including John Lennon and John Betjeman have been known to visit the storied bar Ye Cracke. It offers a wide variety of beers, ales, and ciders in a warm, rustic environment. For history aficionados and those looking for a genuine pub experience, this is the place to go.

2. The Shipping Forecast

15 Slater Street, Liverpool, England, L1 4BW
The Shipping Forecast is a well-known tavern that is situated in the heart of the city. It provides a laid-back ambiance, warm service, and a wide range of artisan spirits, cocktails, and beers. The pub also has DJ nights and live music events, making it a popular choice for a buzzy evening out.

3. Berry & Rye

48 Berry Street, Liverpool, England, L1 4JQ
Berry & Rye, a speakeasy-themed establishment tucked away on Berry Street, is a hidden treasure renowned for its extensive cocktail menu. This little bar's snug and chic atmosphere is complemented by the talented mixologists who craft its delectable and unique beverages. Due to limited capacity, reservations are advised.

4. The Grapes

60 Roscoe Street, Liverpool, England, L1 9DW
The Grape is a classic tavern with a long history that dates back to the 19th century. The establishment serves a variety of authentic ales, beers, and pub favorites in a friendly and inviting environment. The pub is a well-liked place to unwind and have a pint because of its pleasant ambiance and welcoming staff.

5. The Ship & Mitre

133 Dale Street, Liverpool, England, L2 2JH
A classic bar, The Ship & Mitre is well-known for its extensive global beer variety. Beer lovers will find themselves in heaven with the availability of more than 200 different ales and lagers. The bar is popular among beer experts since it frequently holds beer festivals and tasting activities.

6. The Dispensary

87 Renshaw Street, Liverpool, England, L1 2SP
The Dispensary is a nice bar with a laid-back ambiance that emphasizes quality ales and artisan brews. It boasts an inviting interior with charming original characteristics that contribute to the pleasant atmosphere. As you sip a fine brew, take in the pub's lengthy history.

These neighborhood pubs and bars in Liverpool provide a variety of experiences, from traditional settings to hip cocktail lounges. Liverpool offers a variety of venues to choose from, whether your taste is a bustling bar with live music, a typical pub setting, or a distinctive cocktail experience.

Liverpool's Food Markets and Street Food

Liverpool has a thriving food culture, and the best way to experience it is by visiting the city's food markets and street food stands. Here are several must-visit food markets and street food locations in Liverpool, which include everything from fresh produce and artisanal goods to cuisines from across the world and regional specialties:

1. The Liverpool Central Library Food Market

William Brown Street, Liverpool, England, L3 8EW
The Liverpool Central Library Food Market, which takes place every Thursday, brings together several regional merchants who sell an assortment of delectable foods and handcrafted goods. This market is a food lover's heaven, offering everything from freshly baked products and gourmet cheeses to street food kiosks dishing up delicacies from all over the globe.

2. Baltic Triangle

107 Stanhope Street, Liverpool, England L8 5RE
The busy indoor food market known as the Baltic
Market is housed in the thriving Baltic Triangle
neighborhood and offers a broad variety of street
food vendors. This market provides a vibrant and
energizing ambiance with a community sitting area
and live music. Sample menu items include vegan
treats, wood-fired pizzas, Asian street cuisine, and
gourmet burgers.

3. Cuisine and Drink Festival

Postal Code: L17 1AF Sefton Park, Liverpool
The finest of regional and local cuisine and drink
are featured at the annual Liverpool Cuisine and
Drink Festival, which takes place in Sefton Park.
Numerous food vendors, artisanal producers,
culinary demos, and live entertainment are all
included during the event. It's a wonderful chance

to sample a broad range of foods and explore new sensations.

4. Granby Street Market

Granby Street, Liverpool, England L8 2TU
Every first Saturday of the month, the community-run Granby Street Market is held. Fresh fruit, regional cuisine vendors, and handcrafted crafts are all available there. Discover the market to discover enticing selections for street cuisine and exclusive goods from individual vendors.

5. Bold Street

Bold Street in Liverpool, L1
Bold Street, a busy thoroughfare in Liverpool, is well-known for its varied food scene. Discover a variety of independent cafés, restaurants, and street food sellers selling a variety of international cuisines

as you stroll along this bustling road. It's the ideal location for a quick snack or a leisurely cuisine tour.

6. Duke Street Market

Postal Code: L1 5AS in Liverpool, at 46 Duke Street
Duke Street Market is a hip food market with many different food booths and exhibitors. There is something for every taste, from gourmet burgers and wood-fired pizza to fresh seafood and vegan alternatives. The market's chic and contemporary atmosphere offers a colorful background against which to savor a wide variety of gastronomic pleasures.

7. Farmers' Market at Lark Lane

In Liverpool, at Lark Lane, L17
Every fourth Saturday of the month, the Lark Lane Farmers Market offers a variety of regional foods,

handmade goods, and street food vendors. Sample organic veggies, fresh bread, handcrafted chocolates, and more while taking in the vibrant ambiance of this well-known market.

8. Liverpool One Street Food Market

Address: Liverpool One, Chavasse Park, Liverpool L1 8JQ

The Liverpool One Street Food Market displays a range of street food vendors dishing up delectable and varied cuisines and is situated in the middle of the city. There are many alternatives to satiate your tastes, from gourmet hot dogs and Thai curries to Mexican tacos and sweet delights.

Visit these food markets and street food locations while you are in Liverpool to savor a variety of tastes and gastronomic adventures.

V. DAY TRIPS FROM LIVERPOOL

Exploring Chester

The medieval city of Chester is the ideal place for a fun day trip from Liverpool. Chester, which is nearby and provides a wonderful mix of medieval architecture, Roman heritage, and a lively city feel. Here is a thorough guide to seeing Chester:

How to Get There:

Train: Regular trains operate frequently and take around 40 minutes to reach Chester from Liverpool Lime Street station.
By automobile: Chester is readily accessible by automobile through the M53 freeway, and the city center has several parking lots.
Walls of Chester City:

The most comprehensive city walls in Britain, the renowned Chester City Walls are a great place to start your journey. As you travel the 2-mile circle, take in the beautiful vistas of the city and its monuments.

Church of Chester:

Visit Chester Cathedral, an outstanding example of medieval architecture. Discover the breathtaking interior, be amazed by the medieval carvings, and climb the tower for sweeping views of the city.
Eastgate Timepiece

Don't overlook Chester's most recognizable landmark, the Eastgate Clock. It is a popular picture subject and one of the most photographed clock towers in the whole globe.
Using Rows

Discover the distinctive two-tiered retail galleries called "The Rows," which were once part of a medieval fortification and are now home to a variety of independent stores, boutiques, cafés, and restaurants.

Roman Amphitheater in Chester:

The Chester Roman Amphitheatre, the biggest Roman amphitheater in Britain, allows visitors to go back in time. Discover the ruins of this historic building to learn more about the city's Roman past. Whitby Zoo:

A trip to Chester Zoo is essential whether you're traveling with kids or enjoying animals. One of the best zoos in the UK, it is home to a wide variety of animals from all over the globe in beautifully manicured enclosures.

2. River Dee Cruises

Cruise down the River Dee, which runs through the center of Chester, at your leisure. As you float down the lake, take in the beautiful scenery, discover the history of the city, and unwind.

The Grosvenor Museum

Visit the Grosvenor Museum to learn more about Chester's history, archaeology, and art. Discover its intriguing displays, which include collections of excellent art and antiquities from the Roman era.

Shopping and Eating:

Chester provides a wide variety of eating alternatives, from fancy restaurants providing foreign cuisine to quaint pubs serving hearty pub food. Spend some time discovering the distinctive stores and boutiques that are dispersed around the city center.

Chester Races:

Don't miss the chance to experience the thrill of Chester Races if you happen to be there on race day. The racetrack, which is near the city's core, has several racing meets every year.

Chester is a wonderful day excursion from Liverpool because of its fascinating history, beautiful architecture, and lively environment. Chester has something for everyone, whether you want to see Roman ruins, stroll through picturesque alleyways, or indulge in regional food.

Discover Manchester

Manchester is a great option if you're looking for an adventurous day trip from Liverpool. Manchester has a wide variety of sights and activities to experience and is known for its spectacular architecture, vibrant music scene, and rich industrial past. A thorough itinerary is provided below to help you get the most out of your trip to Manchester:

How to Get There:

By Train: It takes around 45 minutes to go by train from Liverpool's Lime Street station to Manchester Piccadilly.

By Car: Manchester is readily accessible through the M62 freeway, and the city center offers several parking alternatives.

Manchester City Center:
Start your investigation at Manchester's city center.
Explore the variety of shops, boutiques, and
department stores by taking a walk through busy
streets like Market Street.

Manchester Town Hall:
Admire the magnificent Manchester Town Hall, a
marvel of Victorian Gothic architecture. Take a
tour with a guide to see the building's unique
construction and discover its history.

John Rylands Library:
Visit the spectacular neo-Gothic John Rylands
Library, which houses a sizable collection of rare
books and manuscripts. Examine its lovely reading
areas and savor the magnificent architecture.

Manchester Cathedral:

Learn about Manchester Cathedral, a masterpiece of medieval architecture. Visit the church's serene interior, go to a service, and take in the breathtaking stained-glass windows.

The Northern Quarter

Immerse yourself in Manchester's Northern Quarter's dynamic and creative vibe. This hip area is well-known for its independently owned stores, street art, unique eateries, and exciting nightlife. Science and Industry Museum

Visit the Museum of Science and Industry to learn more about Manchester's industrial background. Discover the city's contributions to industry, science, and technology via hands-on displays and relics from the past.

The Whitworth Art Gallery

The Whitworth Art Gallery, renowned for its sizable collection of modern and contemporary art, is a great place to enjoy art. Explore the gallery's many displays while strolling around the lovely park setting.

Old Trafford

Football fans should take advantage of the chance to visit Old Trafford, the storied home field of Manchester United. Explore the stadium, stop by the museum, and discover the fascinating history of the team by going on a guided tour.

Manchester Art Gallery

View the remarkable collection of great art that spans centuries at the Manchester Art Gallery.

Admire the creations of well-known artists and peruse the gallery's changing exhibits.

The Lowry

Travel to Salford Quays and check out The Lowry, a thriving arts-focused cultural hub. Take in shows, exhibits, and seminars featuring a variety of creative mediums.

Food and beverage:

Manchester has a vibrant food culture with a wide variety of eateries, cafés, and pubs. Enjoy a culinary trip at one of the numerous popular restaurants in the city, which provide everything from foreign cuisine to regional specialties.

Manchester is a fantastic day trip destination from Liverpool because of its vibrant environment, cultural attractions, and architectural marvels.

Manchester has plenty to offer everyone, whether they are interested in history, art, music, or just soaking in the dynamic spirit of the city.

Explore The Wirral Peninsula

The Wirral Peninsula is an undiscovered treasure worth discovering if you're searching for a gorgeous day trip from Liverpool. This breathtaking area, which spans the Mersey and Dee rivers, provides picturesque coasts, quaint villages, and fascinating history. Listed below is a thorough guide to help you get the most out of your trip to the Wirral Peninsula:

How to Get There:

By Train: Depending on your destination, trains operate frequently from Liverpool Lime Street station to several locations on the Wirral Peninsula. The travel time varies from 15 to 40 minutes.

By automobile: The M53 highway makes it simple to go to the Wirral Peninsula by automobile. In the cities and tourist destinations all around the peninsula, there are several parking possibilities.

West Kirby

Start your journey at the charming seaside village of West Kirby. Take a stroll along the promenade, see the Dee Estuary, and engage in water sports in the marine lake.

Hawaiian Islands

Explore the Hilbre Islands, a collection of tiny islands off the coast of West Kirby. These islands, which are reachable at low tide, provide a unique animal experience and breathtaking natural beauty. Port Sunshine:

Visit Port Sunlight, a quaint town distinguished by its restored architecture and lovely gardens. Discover the history of the community and William Lever's impact by visiting the Port Sunlight Museum.

Wirral Country Park:

At the Wirral Country Park, take in the natural splendor of the Wirral Peninsula. This vast park has trees, walking and cycling routes, and breathtaking views of the Dee Estuary.

Ness Botanic Gardens:

Experience the serenity of Ness Botanic Gardens, a horticultural wonderland with a vast array of plants, flowers, and calm vistas. Take strolls while admiring the colorful exhibits.

Birkenhead Park:

Discover Birkenhead Park, one of the world's earliest public parks and a shining example of Victorian park architecture. Enjoy a leisurely walk around the lovely lake, relax on the grass, and take in the park's historical highlights.

Port Sunlight Garden Village and Museum:

Visit the Port Sunlight Museum to learn more about the city's past. Learn about the Lever Brothers' influence, the village's distinctive architecture, and the region's social history.

The New Brighton

Visit New Brighton, a well-liked beach town with a bustling promenade and breathtaking views of the Mersey River. Enjoy sights including the Marine

Point complex, Fort Perch Rock, and the New
Brighton Lighthouse.

Heswall:

Discover the charming shops, cafés, and eateries in
the town of Heswall. Take a walk through the
lovely Heswall Dales, or dine at Sheldrakes
Restaurant and Bar for views of the Dee Estuary.

Thurstaston Common:

Discover Thurstaston Common's splendor, a
nature reserve with breathtaking views, forest walks,
and a wealth of species. Go for a leisurely trek and
take in the tranquil scenery.

Shopping and Dining:

The Wirral Peninsula has a variety of eating
establishments, including small tearooms, seafood

restaurants, and traditional pubs providing substantial meals. For one-of-a-kind trinkets and handcrafted goods, peruse the stores and boutiques in the area.

The Wirral Peninsula is a great day excursion from Liverpool because of its scenic surroundings, quaint villages, and fascinating history. The Wirral Peninsula offers activities for all tastes, whether you're looking for a calm retreat, cultural events, or beach hikes.

Exploring North Wales

North Wales is an alluring location if you're looking for a breathtaking day trip from Liverpool that offers gorgeous landscapes, historic castles, and rich Welsh history. Here is a detailed itinerary to help you get the most out of your trip to North Wales:

How to Get There:

Train: There are frequent trains from Liverpool Lime Street station to several locations in North Wales. Depending on your destination, travel times might vary; popular stations include Conwy, Llandudno, and Bangor.

By automobile: The A55 and other main highways make it simple to go to North Wales by automobile. In the towns and tourist destinations around the area, there are several parking possibilities.

Conwy Palace

Conwy, a lovely town surrounded by the renowned Conwy Castle, is a good place to start your journey. Explore the picturesque alleyways dotted with shops and cafés, meander around the town walls, and see this historic stronghold.

Snowdonia National Park:

Discover the beautiful panorama of mountains, lakes, and forests in Snowdonia National Park. Take a hike up Mount Snowdon, Wales' tallest mountain, or explore the park on leisurely hikes or picturesque drives.

Llandudno:

Visiting Llandudno, a posh promenade, sandy beaches, and the Great Orme headland are some of the attractions of this Victorian coastal town. Take a trip on the famed Llandudno Cable Car or ride the Great Orme Tramway to take in the expansive vistas.

Portmeirion:

Discover the distinctive Portmeirion, a bright and charming Italianate hamlet tucked away on the shore. Enjoy the calm surroundings while admiring the architecture and strolling around the grounds.

Caernarfon Castle:

Admire Caernarfon Castle, one of Wales' most magnificent castles and a UNESCO World Heritage Site. Discover its impressive walls, towers, and inner courtyard as you discover the rich history of this place.

Bodnant Garden

Experience the splendor of Bodnant Garden, a famous National Trust building. Explore its magnificent gardens, which are home to a wide variety of trees, flowers, and gorgeous vistas of the Conwy Valley.

Anglesey:

Go to the island of Anglesey, which sits off the coast of North Wales. Discover the picturesque coastline and beaches while seeing the ancient town of Beaumaris, which has a medieval castle and quaint alleyways.

Highland Railway in Wales:

Start your adventure on the Welsh Highland Railway for a beautiful train ride. As the steam train carries you through the stunning scenery of Snowdonia National Park, soak in the amazing vistas.

Conwy Suspension Bridge:

Cross the renowned Conwy Suspension Bridge, a significant structure created by Thomas Telford.

View the river and the surroundings from this magnificent feat of engineering.

Welsh Heritage and Culture

Visit regional museums and cultural destinations to learn more about local Welsh history. Visit places like the National Slate Museum and St Fagans National Museum of History to learn more about the Welsh language, customs, and history.

Shopping and Dining:

From upscale dining establishments providing modern cuisine to traditional Welsh pubs serving regional specialties, North Wales provides a variety of eating alternatives. Discover regional markets and artisan stores to find one-of-a-kind trinkets and authentic Welsh goods.

North Wales is a riveting day trip location from Liverpool due to its stunning landscapes, historical landmarks, and rich cultural history. North Wales offers plenty to offer everyone, whether they are looking for outdoor experiences, castle discovery, or a taste of Welsh culture.

Lake District Tour

The Lake District is a great option for a picturesque and relaxing day excursion from Liverpool. The Lake District, well-known for its beautiful vistas, tranquil lakes, and charming towns, provides a tranquil escape from nature. A thorough itinerary is provided below to help you get the most out of your trip to the Lake District:

How to Get There:

Train: There are frequent trains from Liverpool Lime Street station to several Lake District locations. Depending on your location, the travel duration varies; popular stations include Windermere, Kendal, and Ambleside.

By automobile: The M6 highway makes it simple to go to the Lake District by automobile. In the towns and tourist destinations around the area, there are several parking possibilities.

Windermere Lake

The biggest lake in England, Lake Windermere, is a good place to start your tour. Hire a rowing boat or go on a picturesque boat tour to discover the lake's splendor. Take walks along the water's edge and explore Bowness-on-Windermere, a lovely village.

Grasmere:

Visit the Grasmere village, known for its association with the poet William Wordsworth. Explore

Wordsworth's old home, Dove Cottage, and stroll around the small hamlet noted for its tea shops.

The Scafell Pike

For those who like the great outdoors, test yourself by hiking up Scafell Pike, the highest hill in England. As you approach the peak, take in the expansive vistas of the valleys and mountains that surround you.

Derwentwater:

Learn about the splendor of Derwentwater, a gorgeous lake surrounded by picturesque scenery. Enjoy a leisurely boat ride or a stroll along the lakefront while soaking in the peace of the area.

Keswick:

On the beaches of Derwentwater, discover the quaint market town of Keswick. Learn about the history of the region and explore the town's shops and cafés by going to the Keswick Museum and Art Gallery.

Ullswater:

Discover Ullswater's tranquility, another lovely lake in the Lake District. Take a picturesque boat trip, go hiking along the Ullswater Way, or just unwind and take in the tranquility.

Castlerigg Stone Circle:

Admire the ethereal Castlerigg Stone Circle, a Neolithic structure with sweeping vistas of the nearby fells. Take in the spiritual atmosphere by visiting this historic location.

Ambleside:

At the northernmost point of Lake Windermere, discover Ambleside. Take strolls along the lakefront, explore the town's galleries and boutiques, and stop by the lovely Bridge House.

Beatrix Potter Hill Top:

Visit Hill Top, where renowned children's author Beatrix Potter once lived. Investigate the home and grounds that inspired her cherished Peter Rabbit stories and other wonderful characters.

Consterton Water

Learn about the splendor of Coniston Water, a serene lake surrounded by breathtaking scenery. Take a boat ride, take a stroll along the beach, or go to Coniston's neighboring Ruskin Museum.

Shopping and Dining:

The Lake District has a variety of eating establishments, from quaint pubs offering filling meals to fine dining establishments highlighting regional cuisine. Look around local stores for one-of-a-kind items, such as handicrafts, artwork, and native foods.

The Lake District is the perfect day excursion from Liverpool due to its stunning landscape, tranquil lakes, and attractive towns. The Lake District offers activities for all interests, whether you're looking for outdoor adventures, cultural encounters, or a quiet getaway in nature.

VI. SPORTS IN LIVERPOOL

If you're a football fan, a trip to Liverpool wouldn't be complete if you didn't take in some of the city's thriving football scene. Here is a detailed guide to help you make the most of your time spending time with Liverpool FC and Everton FC, two-storied and highly rival football teams located in Liverpool:

Liverpool FC:

- Take a guided stadium tour at Anfield, the renowned home field of Liverpool FC, to follow in the footsteps of football greats, see the locker rooms, and even get up close and personal with the infamous "This Is Anfield" sign.

- At the club's museum, you can fully immerse yourself in the accomplishments and history of Liverpool FC. Discover interactive displays, memorabilia, and information on the club's illustrious players, memorable games, and trophies.

- Experience the electrifying atmosphere of a Liverpool FC game at Anfield if you're fortunate enough to be in Liverpool on a matchday. Join tens of thousands of fervent supporters as they shout well-known chants and support their side.

- Visit the Shankly Gates and Paisley Gates, which are situated outside of Anfield, to pay respects to the illustrious Liverpool FC managers Bill Shankly and Bob Paisley.

Everton FC:

- Take a guided tour of Goodison Park Stadium to get access to the backstage areas, view the locker rooms, and discover the fascinating history of Everton FC.

- Visit the Everton FC Museum to learn more about the history of the team. Explore the exhibitions that highlight the team's historic history and learn about the club's victories and memorable events.

- Matchday Experience: If you have the chance, go to a game at Goodison Park to take in the fervent atmosphere created by the team's devoted supporters. Participate in the cheers and take in the energy on the field.

- Visit the Dixie Dean Statue outside Goodison Park to pay respects to Everton

FC's all-time leading scorer. Take a picture and discover more about the club's illustrious player.

Sports Memorabilia Stores:
stay at official club stores or independent shops to get unique gifts to remember your stay. Explore the football memorabilia shops in Liverpool, where you can purchase merchandise, jerseys, scarves, and other things relating to both Liverpool FC and Everton FC.

Bars and pubs with a football theme:

Visit Liverpool's football-themed clubs and pubs to take in the city's vibrant football vibe. These places have memorabilia all over them, big screens to watch games on, and a terrific atmosphere to talk football with other fans.

The Derby on the Mersey:

Be sure to see this spectacular game if you're lucky enough to be in Liverpool during a Merseyside Derby, the fierce rivalry between Liverpool FC and Everton FC. Visit the stadium to experience the electric atmosphere or watch the game with locals at cafes and pubs.

Walking football tours:

Visit Liverpool's football history by taking a guided walking tour. The clubs, their histories, and the influence they have had on the city's culture are all covered in these excursions as they take you to major football-related locations in the city.

Exploring Liverpool's football teams, stadiums, and fan culture is a worthwhile experience since the city has a strong football culture. Liverpool provides a riveting tour into the heart of the beautiful game, regardless of whether you're a fan of Liverpool FC, Everton FC, or just want to immerse yourself in the passion of football.

Other Sports and Activities

Liverpool has a variety of different sports and events for fans and tourists to enjoy in addition to football. You may check out the following well-liked sports and activities in Liverpool:

- Golf: Liverpool has several top-notch golf courses where you may play a round. The Open tournament has often been held at the famed Royal Liverpool Golf Club in Hoylake.

- Water Sports: Liverpool has chances for a variety of water sports due to its proximity to the shore and the River Mersey. You may take up sailing classes or try your hand at kayaking, paddleboarding, jet skiing, etc.

- Running and cycling are both great activities in Liverpool's many parks, trails, and promenades. Popular options with attractive pathways and well-kept walkways include Sefton Park and Calderstones Park.

- Tennis: If you like playing tennis, you may use the public tennis courts in many parks in Liverpool. For a casual game, consider using the equipment at Wavertree Playground or Calderstones Park.

- Horse Racing: On the outskirts of Liverpool, at Aintree Racecourse, take in the excitement of horse racing. Aintree conducts race meetings all year long and is well known for staging the renowned Grand National steeplechase.

- Fitness & gyms: Make use of Liverpool's fitness facilities to stay in shape while you're there. Modern facilities for courses and exercises are offered by a lot of hotels and recreation areas.

- Indoor sports: If the weather is bad, you may still participate in activities like indoor climbing, trampoline parks, and indoor racing, which are thrilling for people of all ages.

- Parks & Recreation: Liverpool has a lot of parks and green areas where you can relax and engage in leisurely pursuits like picnics and frisbee while taking in the breathtaking scenery. Popular options include Sefton Park and Croxteth Country Park.

- Join exercise courses provided by neighborhood studios and gyms. There are many alternatives to suit different interests and fitness levels, ranging from yoga and Pilates to high-intensity interval training (HIIT) and dance exercises.

- Combat sports and martial arts: Liverpool has a thriving martial arts community with clubs and dojos teaching lessons in mixed martial arts (MMA), Brazilian Jiu-Jitsu, Muay Thai, and boxing.

- Team Sports: If you like team sports, you may play in or watch local competitions in sports like basketball, hockey, cricket, and rugby. Teams and clubs from Liverpool compete in many leagues and tournaments.

- Sports Events: Keep a lookout for any sports events that are taking place while you are there. Every year, Liverpool holds sports events that provide people the chance to participate or watch, including marathons, triathlons, and charity runs.

Liverpool provides a wide variety of activities to occupy sports fans, whether they choose physically demanding indoor activities or outdoor ones. Utilize the city's amenities, parks, and sports organizations to keep active and involved while visiting Liverpool.

VII. LIVERPOOL'S FESTIVALS AND EVENTS

Liverpool is a city renowned for its thriving and diversified cultural scene, and it regularly holds several festivals and events that highlight the city's illustrious history, gifted artists, and vivacious energy. There is always something going on in Liverpool to attract residents and tourists alike, from music and art festivals to cultural festivities and athletic events. The following are some of the best celebrations and events to attend:

LIMF, or the Liverpool International Music Festival

A variety of musical styles are celebrated during the yearly LIMF festival, which takes place in Sefton Park. On several stages, it showcases live performances by well-known performers, up-and-coming musicians, and regional bands. LIMF provides a diverse musical experience to suit all interests, ranging from pop and rock to jazz, R&B, and classical music.

Liverpool Biennial:

The Liverpool Biennial, which takes place every two years, is the biggest festival of contemporary art in the UK. With installations, displays, and performances by international artists, the city is transformed into an outdoor art gallery. Visit the city's galleries, museums, and streets to see thought-provoking and avant-garde artwork.

Worldwide Beatles Week:

Celebrate The Beatles, Liverpool's most well-known export, during International Beatleweek. This festival comprises live music concerts, exhibits, tours, and special activities honoring the Fab Four, drawing Beatles enthusiasts from all around the globe. Relive the enchantment of the Beatles' legacy by immersing yourself in the city's Beatlemania.

Africa Oyé:

The greatest free festival of African and Caribbean music and culture in the UK is called Oyé. This event, which takes place in Sefton Park, has live music, dancing acts, food stands, and a bustling market. In a happy, welcoming environment, take in the rhythms and melodies of Africa and the Caribbean.

Liverpool Pride:

Liverpool Pride is an annual event that celebrates the LGBTQ+ population in the city and encourages equality and diversity. A vibrant procession through the streets of the city, live music, dance acts, and a variety of activities that support LGBTQ+ rights are all part of the celebration.

Grand National

One of the most important horse racing competitions in the world, the Grand National is held at Aintree Racecourse. Watch the competition between riders and their mounts in this renowned steeplechase and feel the thrill and adrenaline. As the action-packed races take place during the event, join the audience and put your bets.

Fireworks Display at Merseyside

The River Mersey is illuminated by the magnificent River of Light fireworks show, which takes place on the waterfront. This yearly celebration mixes fireworks, light shows, music, and entertainment to provide a breathtaking visual extravaganza for everyone to enjoy. Take in the magnificent show from a vantage point along the shoreline.

Liverpool International Theatre Festival:

The Liverpool International Theatre Festival gathers theater groups from all around the globe to display their skills. As foreign theater companies travel to the city's stages, enjoy a wide variety of acts, from drama and comedy to musicals and experimental theater.

The Chinese New Year

The Chinese New Year festivities in Liverpool are among the biggest outside of Asia. Fireworks, traditional lion and dragon dances, vivid street fairs, and colorful parades bring the city to life. Experience authentic Chinese cuisine, take in the festive ambiance, and immerse yourself in the culture.

Food and Drink Festival in Liverpool:

At the Liverpool Food and Drink Festival, which celebrates the gastronomic wonders of the city, indulge your senses. Find a variety of food vendors, regional suppliers, culinary classes, and tasting events. Taste delectable foods, handcrafted goods, and Liverpool's tastes.

These are just a handful of the many festivals and events that Liverpool hosts every year. As you plan your vacation, keep an eye on the city's events schedule to remain current. Liverpool's festivals and events provide a lovely experience that will leave you with priceless memories, whether you're a fan of music, art, or sports, or just want to immerse yourself in the city's lively culture.

VIII. PLANNING YOUR ITINERARY

Recommended Itinerary for a Weekend Trip

Day 1:

Morning:

- When you get there, check into your lodging in Liverpool.

- At a nearby café or restaurant, start your day with a full breakfast.

Mid-Morning:

- Start your city excursion with a trip to the famous Albert Dock. Admire the beautiful waterfront while exploring the different sights, such as Tate Liverpool, the Beatles

Story Museum, and the Merseyside Maritime Museum.

Lunch:

- Enjoy a delectable lunch at one of the Albert Docks eateries or cafés, which provide a variety of cuisines to suit your palate.

Afternoon:

- Enjoy the breathtaking views of the River Mersey by taking a leisurely walk along the charming Liverpool Waterfront.

- One of the city's most stunning architectural wonders, the Liverpool Cathedral, should be seen. Learn about its fascinating history while exploring the inside and climbing the tower for sweeping views.

Evening:

- Go to the thriving Baltic Triangle neighborhood, which is renowned for its independent enterprises and artistic atmosphere. Discover the street art, peruse the specialty stores, and have a beverage at one of the hip pubs or microbreweries.

- Choose from the many restaurants in the Baltic Triangle for supper, which offers a variety of cuisines and creative meals.

Day 2:

Morning:

- Take a guided tour of the storied Anfield Stadium, the home of Liverpool FC, to get a behind-the-scenes look at the club's past and experience the atmosphere first thing in the morning.

Mid-Morning:

- Discover the amazing exhibits at the International Museum Liverpool, which has displays of science, international cultures, and natural history. Explore historical treasures, and engaging exhibits, and discover Liverpool's maritime legacy.

Lunch:

- The city center is a great place to have a leisurely lunch since there are so many restaurants, cafés, and diners there serving a wide range of cuisines.

Afternoon:

- Explore the band's past and the locations connected to their rise to popularity by going on a tour with a Beatles theme. Visit Strawberry Field, Penny Lane, the Cavern Club, and other important Beatles locations.

Evening:

- Discover Liverpool's thriving nightlife in the heart of the city. Discover the vibrant taverns, pubs, and music venues where you can see live shows by regional bands and performers.

Enjoy a delicious supper at one of the city's top-rated eateries, which offers a variety of delectable dishes to satisfy every appetite.

Day 3:

Morning:

- Visit Chester, which is a neighboring city, for a quick excursion. Visit the medieval Chester Cathedral, stroll around the old city walls, and explore the historic Chester Rows. Don't pass up the opportunity to browse the distinctive individual stores and indulge in a classic afternoon tea.

Afternoon:

- Once back in Liverpool, spend the day strolling around the area's cultural hub around William Brown Street. Visit the Central Library, the World Heritage-listed St. George's Hall, and the Walker Art Gallery.

Evening:

- Take a leisurely sail along the Mersey River to round off your weekend getaway. As you cruise around the river, take in the beautiful scenery, discover Liverpool's maritime history, and relax.

This suggested schedule is provided to assist you in organizing your weekend vacation to Liverpool. You are welcome to change it to suit your tastes, the time of year, and the hours when the attractions are open. To guarantee a smooth and pleasurable vacation, be sure to verify the availability of excursions and activities in advance.

Liverpool One Week Itinerary

Day 1:

- Once you get there, relax at your lodging in Liverpool.

- Visit famous sites in the city center, including the Liver Building and St. George's Hall.

- Dinner may be had at a neighborhood restaurant after a walk around the old waterfront.

Day 2:

- Visit the Albert Dock, where the Beatles Story Museum and other attractions are located, to start your day.

- Examine the Tate Liverpool and the Merseyside Maritime Museum.

- Visit a restaurant in Albert Dock for lunch.

- Visit the World Museum Liverpool in the afternoon to discover more about science, global cultures, and natural history.

- Discover the fashionable Baltic Triangle shops and restaurants for supper and nighttime entertainment.

Day 3:

- Visit Chester, a neighboring ancient city renowned for its Roman walls, medieval architecture, and distinctive retail opportunities, for the whole day.

- Discover the Eastgate Clock, the Rows, and Chester Cathedral.

- In one of the lovely tea shops, take pleasure in a classic afternoon tea.

- In the evening, return to Liverpool and unwind at a neighborhood bar or pub.

Day 4:

- Join a tour with a Beatles theme to see locations including Strawberry Field, Penny Lane, and the Cavern Club.

- Learn about the band's background and impact by visiting the Beatles Story Museum.

- Take in a supper with a Beatles theme or go to a concert featuring their songs.

Day 5:

- Visit the adjacent city of Manchester for a day excursion to take in its cultural landmarks including the Science and Industry Museum and the Manchester Art Gallery.

- Visit the thriving Northern Quarter and have lunch at one of the area's hip cafés or eateries.

- Visit Manchester United's home stadium, Old Trafford Stadium, for a tour or a game, if either is offered.

- In the evening, return to Liverpool and unwind at a neighborhood restaurant or bar.

Day 6:

- Discover the area surrounding William Brown Street which is the city's cultural center.

- Visit the World Museum Liverpool, the Central Library, and the Walker Art Gallery.

- Lunch may be had at one of the neighborhood cafés or eateries.

- Visit the Liverpool Cathedral in the afternoon and climb the tower for sweeping views of the city.

- Spend the evening eating at a riverside restaurant at the Royal Albert Dock and taking in the lively ambiance.

Day 7:

- Enjoy the beautiful scenery by taking a leisurely sail along the River Mersey.

- Take a tour of Anfield Stadium and the Liverpool Football Club Museum.

- Discover Liverpool's lively nightlife by visiting its pubs, clubs, and live music venues.

- Attend a goodbye dinner at a renowned restaurant in the area.

Note: This travel schedule offers a broad overview of a week-long journey to Liverpool. You are welcome to change it to suit your tastes and preferences. To guarantee a seamless and pleasurable vacation, check the opening times and accessibility of sites, excursions, and events beforehand.

Customizing Your Itinerary

Day 1:

- Discover the city's historic district and stop by sites including St. George's Hall and the Liver Building.

- If you like history, you may want to check out the Victoria Gallery & Museum or the Museum of Liverpool.

- Spend the day at the Walker Art Gallery or the Tate Liverpool if you're an art enthusiast.

Day 2:

- Take a tour with a Beatles theme to start your day off, stopping at places like Penny Lane and the Cavern Club.

- If you like sports, take a tour of Anfield Stadium to learn more about the history of Liverpool FC.

- Alternatively, go to Goodison Park Stadium if you're an Everton supporter.

Day 3:

- Visit Chester for the day; it's a historic city with Roman walls and interesting shopping.

- Discover the Rows, and Chester Cathedral, and take part in a traditional afternoon tea.

- Visit the Dewa Roman Experience and the Roman Amphitheater if you're interested in Roman history.

Day 4:

- Visit the Merseyside Maritime exhibit and the Beatles Story exhibit while spending the morning at the Albert Dock.

- Explore the thriving Baltic Triangle neighborhood in the afternoon to see its small stores, street art, and microbreweries.

Day 5:

- Spend the day discovering Liverpool's live music scene if you like music. For classical music events, check out small-scale venues like the Jacaranda or the Philharmonic Hall.

- Alternatively, go to the British Music Experience or the Liverpool Philharmonic Hall to learn more about the city's extensive musical history.

Day 6:

- If you want to see another energetic city, take a day excursion to Manchester. Visit cultural sites like the Science and Industry Museum or the Manchester Art Gallery.

- Explore the fashionable Northern Quarter's distinctive boutiques and cafés while enjoying lunch there.

- Upon your return, spend the evening taking in Liverpool's nightlife.

Day 7:

- If you're a fan of the outdoors, check out the city's parks and green areas, such as Sefton Park or Calderstones Park.

- Spend the day visiting Liverpool ONE, a sizable retail center with a variety of stores and restaurants, if you prefer shopping.

- Attend a show at the Royal Court Theatre or the Liverpool Empire Theatre in the evening.

Note: Depending on your interests, you may tailor your week-long vacation to Liverpool using the options in this itinerary. To design an itinerary that meets your interests, feel free to combine and contrast the sights and activities. Make careful to confirm the accessibility and operating times of attractions and activities in advance.

IX. PRACTICAL INFORMATION AND TIPS

Money-Saving Tips

• Plan and make reservations: Look for early bird specials on travel, lodging, and activities. You may get better rates and save money when you make reservations in advance.

• Use the trains and buses that Liverpool has to offer; it boasts a sizable public transit system. Use these methods as an alternative to taxis or rental vehicles to move about the city and save money on transportation.

• The museums and galleries at the Albert Dock, the Walker Art Gallery, and the World Museum Liverpool are just a few of the free attractions Liverpool has to offer. Utilize these chances to discover the city's culture without paying a dime.

- Consider bringing a picnic and eating it in one of Liverpool's parks or green areas rather than eating out every time. This enables you to experience the gorgeous areas of the city while saving money on meals.

- In Liverpool, several restaurants and pubs provide happy hours and meal discounts. Take advantage of these special offers to enjoy reduced-priced food and beverages.

- Check for any discount cards or coupons that are offered by Liverpool's tourist destinations, eateries, and stores. These may result in considerable cost savings on shopping, meals, and admission fees.

- Visit local markets: You may discover cheap, excellent food, fresh produce, and interesting gifts at local markets like the one at the Liverpool Central Library or the one at St. John's Shopping Centre.

- Think about inexpensive lodging: Look for Liverpool hostels or guesthouses that are affordable. These choices often provide relaxing stays for a small portion of the price of expensive hotels.

- Avoid staying in the city center since the cost of hotels is often greater there. Consider reserving a place to stay in Liverpool's suburbs, where prices are often cheaper, and then using public transit to work.

- Making use of free walking tours is a terrific way to see Liverpool's sites and learn about its history without having to pay for guided excursions.

Keep in mind that you shouldn't sacrifice your experience to save money. You can maximize your vacation to Liverpool while staying within your budget with little forward preparation and the help of these money-saving suggestions.

Helpful Websites and Apps

Websites:

- Visit Liverpool (www.visitliverpool.com): The city of Liverpool's official tourist website offers in-depth details on attractions, events, lodging, and insider advice.

- Merseytravel (www.merseytravel.gov.uk): This website provides information about Liverpool's public transportation, such as bus and rail timetables, ticket costs, and travel updates.

- The popular travel website TripAdvisor (www.tripadvisor.com) offers evaluations, suggestions, and rankings for hotels, eateries, activities, and more in Liverpool.

- Liverpool Echo (www.liverpoolecho.co.uk): A local news website where you can discover advice on what to do and see in Liverpool, as well as news from the area.

Apps:

- The official Visit Liverpool app for iOS and Android gives thorough information about attractions, events, maps, and special offers and discounts.

- You may explore Liverpool's bus and rail lines with the aid of Citymapper (iOS, Android), a comprehensive public transportation software that offers real-time updates and instructions.

- The TripAdvisor app (iOS, Android) gives you access to reviews, ratings, and suggestions while you're on the move, making it easier for you to discover the top places to dine, stay, and visit in Liverpool.

- National Rail Enquiries (iOS, Android): This app offers real-time train timetables, ticket pricing, and travel updates for the full UK rail network if you want to travel by train outside of Liverpool.

- Uber is a transportation service that operates in Liverpool and is available on iOS and Android devices.

These online resources and mobile applications will help you with vacation preparation, city navigation, attraction discovery, and information upkeep. Keep in mind to verify that these applications are accessible and compatible with your device and location before downloading them.

Safety and Health Tips

- Keep an eye on your surroundings: It's crucial to be cautious and aware of your surroundings in any city, particularly when it's busy or late at night. Be careful not to expose expensive goods, and keep your possessions safe.

- Use dependable transportation: Choose authorized taxis or respectable ride-sharing services like Uber. When using public transit, be careful with your possessions and stay away from busy places during rush hours.

- Keep current with the most recent COVID-19 rules in Liverpool by following the recommendations. Follow social distancing practices, if necessary, wear masks in public areas, and wash your hands often to maintain proper hygiene.

- Taking good care of your personal property includes keeping items like passports, wallets, and phones locked up at all times. To avoid carrying a lot of cash, carry just what you need in a money belt or safe bag.

- Contact information for your country's embassy or consulate, emergency services (call 999 in an emergency), and your lodging should all be saved in case of an emergency. Find out where the closest medical centers and hospitals are.

- Carry a water bottle with you and make sure to drink enough water, particularly in hot weather, to stay hydrated and protect yourself from the sun. For sun protection, use sunscreen and don a hat or sunglasses.

- Ensure you have enough prescription medicine for the length of your trip if you must carry any medication. In case of an emergency, have a copy of your medications or other medical records with you and look for local hospitals or clinics.

- Respect local laws and traditions: To guarantee that you conduct yourself properly and stay out of trouble with the law, familiarize yourself with the local traditions and laws. When visiting holy places, dress modestly and show sensitivity to cultural differences.

- Keep in touch: Inform crucial contacts of your location and goals. Give friends or family members a copy of your itinerary, and keep in touch with them often while traveling.

- Travel insurance: Think about getting travel insurance that provides coverage for lost or stolen luggage, medical emergencies, and trip cancellations. To be sure the insurance satisfies your requirements, review the specifics.

Remember that these are just basic recommendations, so it's always a good idea to look up particular safety and health data relevant to your intended trip. To have a secure and happy vacation to Liverpool, keep informed, use common sense, and put your well-being first.

Packing List for a Trip to Liverpool

Clothing:

- Dress appropriately for the weather: Before your travel, check the weather prediction and bring clothes suited to the climate. Due to Liverpool's variable weather, pack a combination of light and warm clothing.

- Pack a pair of comfortable walking shoes or sneakers since Liverpool is best experienced on foot.

- Liverpool is renowned for its sporadic downpours, so it's a good idea to take a waterproof jacket or umbrella.

- If you want to travel during the summer, think about bringing a swimsuit if you want to cool down in any outdoor pools or at many local beaches.

Travel necessities:

- Make sure you have a current passport as well as any other essential travel documentation, such as a visa.

- Bring a travel adaptor if your gadgets have various plug types since the UK utilizes Type G electrical outlets.

- Carry enough local cash (British pounds) with you, and for convenience, think about carrying a credit or debit card.

- Keep a copy of your travel insurance policy on hand, along with emergency phone numbers.

Accessories and electronics:

- Keep your phone and charger close by for communication and navigation. Don't forget to bring a power bank or charger.

- Use a camera or a smartphone to record recollections.

- Consider taking a portable Wi-Fi device or confirm that your cell plan offers foreign data if you wish to be connected at all times.

Medicines and toiletries

- Personal toiletries: Bring your favorite toiletries, such as your toothbrush, toothpaste, shampoo, conditioner, and any other products you may need for your skin.

- Prescription drugs: Bring a sufficient amount of any prescription drugs you need, as well as a copy of your prescriptions.

Miscellaneous:

- Carry a travel guidebook or use a travel app on your smartphone to help you discover and navigate Liverpool.

- Small day bags or backpacks help transport necessities when visiting a place.

- Snacks and water bottles: Keep yourself hydrated and energetic during the day by carrying snacks and a reusable water bottle.
- Consider bringing travel locks if you'll be staying in a place with lockers or if you want to give your possessions a little more protection.

- Never forget to verify your airline's or the transportation company's particular guidelines for baggage limitations. To guarantee a relaxing and happy vacation to Liverpool, pack thoughtfully and give priority to the things you need.

FAQs about Liverpool

What time of year is ideal for visiting Liverpool?
A: The spring (March to May) and summer (June to August) seasons are ideal for visiting Liverpool because of the moderate weather and plenty of outdoor activities.

What is the best way to go from Liverpool John Lennon Airport to the city center?
A: There are several transportation options to and from Liverpool John Lennon Airport. To get to your location, you may use a cab, an airport shuttle, or public transit like buses or trains.

Are there any Liverpool attractions that are connected to the Beatles?

A: Liverpool is well known for being where The Beatles were born. To learn more about the history and legacy of the Beatles, you may visit places like The Beatles Story Museum, and the Cavern Club, and go on a tour that is themed after them.

What Liverpool museums should you not miss?
A: You may learn about many facets of the history, culture, and art of Liverpool at many renowned museums, including the Museum of Liverpool, the Tate Liverpool, the World Museum of Liverpool, and the Merseyside Maritime Museum.

A day excursion from Liverpool to other surrounding cities is conceivable, right?
A: Yes, day excursions from Liverpool may be taken to places like Chester, Manchester, and even the picturesque Lake District. Trains and buses make it simple to get to these cities.

Are there tours of Liverpool's football stadiums available?

A: Yes, you may take a tour of either Liverpool FC or Everton FC's renowned stadiums, learn about their histories, and view the backstage areas.

Is it safe to stroll around Liverpool after dark?

A: Although Liverpool is a relatively secure city, it is always good to follow standard safety measures. These include staying in populated areas, avoiding remote regions, and being alert to your surroundings, particularly at night.

What Liverpool-specific cuisine should you try?

A: Scouse, a beef stew, Liverpool pies, and seafood specialties like fish and chips or a seafood platter are all considered traditional foods of Liverpool.

A: Can I get about Liverpool using public transportation?

A: Yes, Liverpool boasts a well-functioning public transit system that includes trains and buses, making it simple to travel across the city and take in all of its attractions.

Do any music festivals or other events take place in Liverpool?
A: The Liverpool Sound City Festival, International Beatleweek, and the LIMF (Liverpool International Music Festival) are just a few of the music-related events and festivals that Liverpool stages throughout the year.

X. CONCLUSION

In conclusion, the Liverpool Travel Guide offers an insider's viewpoint and a customized itinerary for a trip to Liverpool that won't soon be forgotten.

Liverpool has plenty to offer for everyone, whether you're a history buff, a football fan, a music aficionado, or just looking for a dynamic and diverse city experience.

From Liverpool's modest origins as a port city to its development into a dynamic cultural center, the tour walks you through the city's rich history. It examines the key sights in the city, such as well-known places associated with the Beatles and the Albert Dock, the Liverpool Cathedral, and other recognizable structures. A sense of the city's genuine charm is also provided via the spotlighting of undiscovered treasures and neighborhood favorites.

The book offers thorough information on the top locations to visit, dine, buy, and relax in Liverpool, covering everything from museums and galleries to parks and gardens, from shopping to nightlife. You may easily organize your vacation with the aid of the useful information it provides on transportation, visa requirements, safety advice, and cost-saving techniques.

Additionally, the book gives suggested itineraries for weekend trips and one-week stays, providing you with a well-organized schedule to make the most of your time in Liverpool. Additionally, it promotes personalization depending on your hobbies, enabling you to adjust your schedule to fit your tastes.

The book makes sure you have a smooth and comfortable stay in Liverpool by providing thorough descriptions, locations, and suggestions for lodging, restaurants, cafés, and pubs. Additionally, it emphasizes the various festivals and events that take place in the city, giving information on Liverpool's cultural calendar.

The Liverpool Travel Guide is a thorough tool that you should use as your go-to travel companion while discovering all that this vibrant city has to offer. This travel guide will enable you to make lasting experiences in Liverpool whether you're a first-time visitor or a seasoned traveler.

Summary of The Guide

The Liverpool Travel Guide offers insider information on one of the UK's most interesting cities. This book provides a thorough examination of Liverpool's history, landmarks, culture, and local favorites and is packed with insider information, in-depth explanations, and tailored itineraries.

The book goes into the core of Liverpool, exploring everything from the city's intriguing past as a maritime powerhouse to its live music scene and strong football culture. It emphasizes the famous monuments that make Liverpool a must-visit location for music lovers, such as the Albert Dock, the Liver Building, and the internationally known Beatles-related attractions.

Beyond the well-known sights, the tour reveals undiscovered jewels and neighborhood hotspots, letting visitors fully experience the city's unique character. Readers will learn about the many experiences that make Liverpool special, from visiting the museums and galleries to wandering through the lovely parks and gardens.

To guarantee a smooth and pleasurable vacation, the book also offers useful information on transportation, visa requirements, safety advice, and cost-saving techniques. Whether visitors have a weekend or a whole week to explore, they can make the most of their time in Liverpool with suggested itineraries for both quick excursions and extended stays.

The book makes sure readers have an enjoyable and memorable trip in Liverpool by providing thorough descriptions, locations, and suggestions for lodging, restaurants, cafés, and pubs. Additionally, it promotes the city's exciting festivals and events, showing the dynamic cultural scene that welcomes guests all year long.

The Liverpool Travel Guide is a thorough guide that combines in-depth local knowledge with useful recommendations, making it a must-have travel companion for anybody organizing a trip to Liverpool. Travelers may set off on an exciting adventure through the history, culture, and vivacious energy of this magnificent city with the aid of this guide.

Printed in Great Britain
by Amazon

44426495R00106